The author and the publishers express their appreciation to the editors of the following periodicals, in the pages of which poems from this book were first published: *The Chariton Review, The Falcon, Field, Lemming, Madrona, Occurrence, Pocket Pal, Poetry Now, Seneca Review, Skywriting, Stooge,* and *Works.*

The author gratefully acknowledges the financial aid given him during the preparation of this book by the Connecticut Foundation for the Arts and the National Endowment for the Arts, and the publishers similarly acknowledge with thanks the support of the A. W. Mellon Foundation toward the publication of this book.

Library of Congress Cataloging in Publication Data

Edson, Russell.
    The reason why the closet-man is never sad.

    (Wesleyan poetry program; v. 84)
    I. Title.
PS3509.D583R4   811'.5'2   76-51444
ISBN 0-8195-2084-5
ISBN 0-8195-1084-X pbk.

Manufactured in the United States of America: First edition

THE REASON WHY THE CLOSET-MAN IS NEVER SAD

The Wesleyan Poetry Program: Volume 84

THE REASON WHY THE CLOSET-MAN IS NEVER SAD

by RUSSELL EDSON

WESLEYAN UNIVERSITY PRESS, MIDDLETOWN, CONNECTICUT

FOR FRANCES

CONTENTS

THE REASON WHY THE CLOSET-MAN IS NEVER SAD

The turtle carries his house on his back. He is both the house and the person of that house.

But actually, under the shell is a little room where the true turtle, wearing long underwear, sits at a little table. At one end of the room a series of levers sticks out of slots in the floor, like the controls of a steam shovel. It is with these that the turtle controls the legs of his house.

Most of the time the turtle sits under the sloping ceiling of his turtle room reading catalogues at the little table where a candle burns. He leans on one elbow, and then the other. He crosses one leg, and then the other. Finally he yawns and buries his head in his arms and sleeps.

If he feels a child picking up his house he quickly douses the candle and runs to the control levers and activates the legs of his house and tries to escape.

If he cannot escape he retracts the legs and withdraws the so-called head and waits. He knows that children are careless, and that there will come a time when he will be free to move his house to some secluded place, where he will relight his candle, take out his catalogues and read until at last he yawns. Then he'll bury his head in his arms and sleep. . . . That is, until another child picks up his house. . . .

11

Aunt Hobbling in her kitchen making a small but shapely breakfast turns and smiles in such a way as to make us aware of the constant space that surrounds her, embracing her, among those things of constant use, things that have become a kind of body music, echoed in the natural sounds of the forest, and in the faint thunders of the distant sky.

She thinks of the finery scarred; rough seductions, as though one could collect a wealth made ugly by breaking through locked doors to those small but shapely interiors. . . . One's feelings numbed now by that inner awareness of all the outward shows of all those small but shapely mercies. . . .

Yet, in the meantime, the dew, like small glass beads, aligns itself with the sun to make those small but shapely pieces in the grass of what we take to be the purity of light. . . . She floats, suddenly enlightened, like a Kleenex in the wind. . . .

Meanwhile, we return once more to the kitchen of Aunt Hobbling, where she turns once more, smiling. And we see her among her things, as part of a collage in which the adhesive withers, so that the piece flutters, or shall we say, shivers, in those small but shapely winds that enter open windows with mercurial desire. . . .

THE AUTOPSY

In a back room a man is performing an autopsy on an old raincoat.

His wife appears in the doorway with a candle and asks, how does it go?

Not now, not now, I'm just getting to the lining, he murmurs with impatience.

I just wanted to know if you found any blood clots?

Blood clots?!

For my necklace. . . .

THE BALLOON OF MEMORY

. . . Even the dead must rise should time endure.

But what if time grows thin and will not hold the next event, bloated out like a spider's web in the winds of change, dotted with the corpses of the too many dead . . . ?

. . . Out there, a balloon of memory: a summer day; the distant hills, like purple blankets on the knees of seated giants. . . .

13

In his travels he comes to a bridge made entirely of bones. Before crossing he writes a letter to his mother: Dear mother, guess what? the ape accidentally bit off one of his hands while eating a banana. Just now I am at the foot of a bone bridge. I shall be crossing it shortly. I don't know if I shall find hills and valleys made of flesh on the other side, or simply constant night, villages of sleep. The ape is scolding me for not teaching him better. I am letting him wear my pith helmet for consolation. The bridge looks like one of those skeletal reconstructions of a huge dinosaur one sees in a museum. The ape is looking at the stump of his wrist and scolding me again. I offer him another banana and he gets very furious, as though I'd insulted him. Tomorrow we cross the bridge. I'll write to you from the other side if I can; if not, look for a sign. . . .

With ceremonial regret I lowered a seed into the earth as though I laid it to its final rest. . . .

If this seed live again then so shall I.

Which, of course, is sheer nonsense placed in the service of a tongue too long in the damp sleep of its mouth.

From a cloud an ancestor looked out at me. And I thought surely a moment had been reached. And I wasn't wrong, a moment had been reached—and then another—minutes, hours—yes, entire time, before and after me, proceeding in orderly fashion, through me and through the trees like sunlight or a fine rain when the air is so lovely. . . .

Had I suddenly become filled with God? Or was it a house falling in upon itself in the distance with a small sigh of dusty desperation? A cloud musty with the smell of old coats. . . . The sound of distant calliopes! The trumpeting of elephants!

15

. . . Standing on a cliff overlooking the sea, sea gulls like scraps of paper blowing over the rocks below. A steady northeast wind, at first refreshing, then chilling; storm coming. . . .

An old fisherman wearing rubber boots makes his way along the cliff. He is carrying something on his back; it is supported by a line over his shoulder which he clutches in his hands. It seems to be a large fish.

On closer inspection it turns out to be an old woman, the line coming out of her open mouth. I imagine a fishhook stuck in her throat.

The old fisherman stops and lets the old woman slide off his back to the ground. Storm coming, he says. He nods in the direction of the old woman on the ground, my wife.

Is she dead? I say, trying to sound concerned.

Oh no, just resting; we always take our walk along the cliffs.

He puts his fingers in her mouth and removes the hook from her throat. There ya be, he sighs.

His wife sits up and yawns; she says, looks like a storm coming.

The old fisherman puts the hook in his mouth and swallows it. And now the old woman picks up the line and begins dragging the old man away. His eyes are shut.

I see the old woman struggling with the line over her shoulder, dragging what seems to be a large fish, as she makes her way through a fine rain just beginning to fall.

THE CLOSET

Here I am with my mother, hanging under the molt of years, in a garden of umbrellas and rubber boots, together always in the vague perfume of her coat.

See how the fedoras along the shelf are the several skulls of my father, in this catacomb of my family.

17

Dr. Glowingly turned to Dr. Glisteningly and said, why are you copying everything I do?

But why are you copying everything I do? replied Dr. Glisteningly.

We can't both be copying, cried Dr. Glowingly.

But I deny it! screamed Dr. Glisteningly.

One of us is copying the other, said Dr. Glowingly.

Admittedly, conceded Dr. Glisteningly, the piling up of coincidence is far too great; either we are both being controlled by a third party, which I rather disbelieve, or one of us is being cued by the other.

I believe you are unconsciously imitating me — no more of it! Dr. Glisteningly; I will not have my spontaneity blurred by your constant echo, said Dr. Glowingly.

Why, look at you, wearing the same deerstalker cap as I wear, the same gray spats, cried Dr. Glisteningly.

Well, it's no secret that I admire your taste — why shouldn't I, isn't it in direct imitation of mine? said Dr. Glowingly.

Perhaps we will not prove who is the copycat, but I do think some effort ought to be made to interrupt this mirror effect of our appearances, particularly the calabash pipes, said Dr. Glisteningly.

I have the corrective, said Dr. Glowingly as he pulled a derringer out of his breast pocket. . . . Even of course as Dr. Glisteningly was also pulling a derringer out of his breast pocket. . . .

THE CONSPIRACY

A fat lady in a circus is fired for losing an ounce of weight. At the same time the thin man is fired for having gained an ounce of weight.

The circus manager thinks the fat lady and the thin man are working a conspiracy.

To make matters worse, the fat lady returns to show the circus manager that she has gained two ounces, even as the thin man returns and shows the circus manager that he has lost two ounces.

The circus manager thinks that somehow they are exchanging ounces.

Oh no, says the circus manager, you're not fooling me, it's a conspiracy disguised as a coincidence, so obviously synchronized for the commission of symmetrical conspiracies.

He has built himself a cottage in a wood, near where the insect rubs its wings in song.

Yet, without measure, or a proper sense of scale, he has made the cottage too small. He realizes this when only his hand will fit through the door.

He tries the stairs to the second floor with his fingers, but his arm wedges in the entrance.

He wonders how he shall cook his dinner. He might get his fingers through the kitchen windows, but even so, the stove's too tiny to cook enough food; the pots are like thimbles and bottle caps.

He must also lie unsheltered in the night even though a tiny bed, with its covers turned down, waits for him in the cottage.

He curls himself around the cottage, listening to the insect that rubs its wings in song. . . .

A little piece of the ape's nostril had fallen off; and then we noticed one of its ears was chipped. On closer examination we saw that one of its fingernails was missing.

By this time, of course, we had grown to love the ape, but still we wondered if it shouldn't be sent back for an undamaged one.

The guarantee slip was still tied to one of its ears: This ape is guaranteed in perfect working order on day of purchase.

But then we noticed something else written on the slip: Floor model, demonstration ape, reduced for quick sale.

Ah, so we did get a bargain without even knowing it.

The ape shyly smiles and presents its cheek for a kiss. . . .

But later on in the evening a large hole develops in the ape's stomach from what had seemed earlier only a tiny tear. And all evening we watched the ape's insides slowly coming out all over the rug. . . .

21

For a while now a woman has been turning into a double bed. She no longer wears regular clothes, but finds bedsheets and covers more fitting and comfortable to her new physical frame.

Her mother and father implore her not to encourage the seeming aspect by wearing bedclothes in the street.

The time was coming when she would no longer be able to leave the house, when she would have to remain in one of the bedrooms.

Her father removed the bed and said, I don't suppose you'll need a bed, because you are yourself a bed.

The family studied her to see just what style of bed she was becoming, so that they might buy matching furniture for her bedroom.

Her mother was afraid that she might be becoming some of that *modern stuff.*

Her father hoped she wouldn't be too old-fashioned, because that would seem too spinsterish.

The woman listens to her father and mother murmuring at night in the room next to hers. Her father murmuring in the dark, perhaps if she had gotten married there would have been a man in her double bed, and she wouldn't have to become a double bed all by herself. Oh, yes, it helps when you're married, it's such a lonely thing for a woman to become a double bed all by herself, murmurs her mother in the dark.

The woman thinks, it's a lot more comfortable, even in a double bed, to be alone.

And she lies alone in her double bed, the double bed she has become, staring up at the ceiling in the dark. . . .

A man sitting in the dark sees through a doorway into a lighted bedroom. Somehow there are two of him. In the bedroom the other of him is packing a suitcase.

When he looks again there's another of him. This one is hopping about the room holding his penis, asking the one packing if he knows where there's a woman.

Before he knows it, a fourth other of him is in the bedroom. This one, paying no attention to the other two, is trying to rearrange the furniture.

Pretty soon the bedroom is full of others of him, some scratching their heads, others pacing; one is crying, another is nursing a baby-bottle. The one holding his penis is still trying to find a woman.

Now the man sitting in the dark becomes aware that there's a crowd of himself sitting in the dark with him, all watching, as he, what is happening in the bedroom.

In the end the one who can't find a woman is ejaculating all over the floor.

The man and the others of him sitting in the dark find this very dreary. . . .

THE DUMMY

A man made a dummy and sat it on a chair with a begging cup. He comes for it at night and drags it up the stairs to his room by its hair, after emptying its begging cup into his pockets.

He gives the dummy a penny: that's for you.

Sometimes he leans out of the window and loops a rope around the dummy's neck and pulls it up into the window.

Sometimes he uses a fishing rod and catches the dummy with a big hook in its breast, and yanks it up through the window.

Sometimes, for variety, he comes with a big stick and beats the dummy until the terrified dummy flees upstairs.

And here's a penny for your trouble.

One day the dummy doesn't work; some kind of dummy-trouble. So the man has got to sit downstairs with the begging cup.

When it is night the dummy leans out the window and throws a loop around the man's neck, and casts a fishing line with a big hook into the man's breast, and pulls the man through the window by his hair.

No no, dummy, I appreciate what you are trying to do, but you are not designed to hurt me.

The dummy empties the begging cup into its pocket and tosses the man a penny.

Thank you, dummy, but I'll take all the money.

The dummy picks up a stick. . . .

No no, dummy, you are not designed to hurt me; I am designed to hurt you. . . .

A father with a huge eraser erases his daughter. When he finishes there's only a red smudge on the wall.

His wife says, where is Amyloo?

She's a mistake, I erased her.

What about all her lovely things? asks his wife.

I'll erase them too.

All her pretty clothes? . . .

I'll erase her closet, her dresser—shut up about Amyloo! Bring your head over here and I'll erase Amyloo out of it.

The husband rubs his eraser on his wife's forehead, and as she begins to forget she says, hummm, I wonder whatever happened to Amyloo? . . .

Never heard of her, says her husband.

And you, she says, who are you? You're not Amyloo, are you? I don't remember your being Amyloo. Are you my Amyloo, whom I don't remember anymore? . . .

Of course not, Amyloo was a girl. Do I look like a girl?

. . . I don't know, I don't know what anything looks like anymore. . . .

The curtains part: it is a summer's day. There a cow on a grassy slope watches as a bull charges an old aeroplane in a meadow. The bull is punching holes with its horns in the aeroplane's fabric . . .

Suddenly the aeroplane's engine ignites; the meadow is dark with blue smoke . . .

The aeroplane shifts round and faces the charging bull.

As the bull comes in the propeller takes off the end of its muzzle. The bloody nostrils, a ring through them, are flung to the grass with a shattered blossom of teeth.

The bull, blood oozing from the stump of its face, backs off, and charges again. This time the propeller catches the bull behind its lower jaw and flings the head into a tree.

The headless bull backs off once more, and then charges down again. The propeller beating at the headless bull, cutting the body away in a great halo of blood, until only the back legs are standing. These run wildly away through the meadow in figure eights and zigzags, until at last they find the aeroplane again. And as they come running down the propeller whacks them apart.

The legs, one with the tail still attached to it, the other somehow retaining both rectum and testicles, scamper off in opposite directions.

The aeroplane turns away; the engine stops.

The shadows are suddenly seen in lengthened form.

The watching cow begins to low . . .

Some people who had been turned into fish—they had been Americans—decided to swim over to Europe.

No no, I want to go to South America, said a female fish who had been a middle-aged woman.

Still, another fish, claiming to have been a butler, thought that they had best remain near the shore of Long Island Sound just in case the metamorphosis didn't fully take, and they were restored back into humanity. Besides, who wants to see foreigners? There is more comfort in watching one's own countrymen on the shore of one's own country.

Yes yes, cried the unhappy fish, let us watch our countrymen.

And so they watched from the waters of Long Island Sound their countrymen on the beaches of Stamford, Connecticut, for as long as larger fish, who had not formerly been human, did not eat them, or their countrymen, in the form of a grandfather and his young grandson, did not catch them on hooks, or, for that matter, as long as they didn't flip themselves up on the beach, absentmindedly forgetting that they were fish, and smothering thus . . .

An old woman bakes a life-sized gingerbread man, whom she immediately marries and lives happily ever after with, save that she's one of those wives who've the habit of picking on their husbands, and putting the pieces in their mouths.

When she notices all the holes it's too late; so she knocks off the rest of him.

— Pounding on the door, two huge gingerbread policemen; they drag her through the night to the gingerbread judge, who orders her to the gingerbread jail.

But she's a clever old woman, and makes a key out of gingerbread and opens the gingerbread lock, and escapes from the gingerbread jail.

But, on the outside, finds everything has turned to gingerbread, the trees, the streets, the people walking in the streets, all made of gingerbread, even rocks and insects. She is the only thing not made of gingerbread . . .

Meanwhile, two gingerbread policemen, with drawn gingerbread guns, full of gingerbread bullets, are chasing her down the gingerbread streets . . .

... I didn't think it would work, the crew was entirely composed of animals.

The captain is a talking dog. If you manipulate his throat while he whines he can make the word *mama*. Is this enough to run a ship?

Then there's a horse who can answer simple addition by stamping one of his hooves.

There's a seal too, who balances a beach ball on his nose, and applauds with his front flippers on command.

I wonder if this is enough of a crew?

Somehow the ship makes its way into the harbor and out to sea. The elephants, in a chain, linked by their tails and trunks, are walking around the deck. The horse is counting something out with its front hoof. A monkey is pushing a little cup at me for money. I fail to see any seamanship in this ...

Then the ship begins to sink. I manipulate the captain's throat that he might issue some emergency orders. But all he can seem to say is *mama*.

Mama, at a time like this?

But the captain seems more interested in a bone he keeps under his bunk.

The elephants continue to parade around the deck. And I can't see why the seal continues to applaud; unless it's because he realizes his good fortune, being the most aquatic of any of us on board.

Then the captain suddenly manages *papa;* maybe he'll be able to find some words of instruction for the crew before it's too late.

The monkey is still pushing its little begging cup at me for money. But even as I manage to find some change the water is coming over the gunwales . . .

Final note: We were all saved, except for the seal, who continued the voyage on his own.

Observation: In my opinion the captain's vocabulary does not recommend him to a position of command, particularly at sea. In my judgment, both the captain and the crew would be better served in a circus; some, even, as house pets . . .

The piano keys are a single board painted to look like keys.

And, oh yes, speaking of keys, the keyhole of a door is found to be merely painted on the door.

Even a key figure in government is found to be something painted on a wall.

And, as you approach the painted keyhole with your key, you discover that your key was made for a sardine can.

Then the key figure, the one painted on the wall, is about to give the keynote address. We are lost!

At last the pianist has arrived, and is about to perform *Pictures at an Exhibition.*

He strikes the painted keyboard and all the piano strings sound at once like a noisy mud, like a huge bell tolling from the center of the earth . . .

A man who is making his way in a city, whose name he has forgotten, suddenly loses his hat to the wind. As it sails to the other side of the street, he whispers, please God, help me to recover my hat.

The hat hits a large building and knocks it down.

The police come.

The man says, but you see, sirs, the wind . . . not to mention the fact that the hat isn't really right for me, something bought rather hastily on my way to catching the train to your city. . . . You would have certainly thought that a man of my taste would've told the hatter, no no, except for my shyness, which had me say, yes yes, how very good of you to see this hat for me . . .

The police say, well, try it on, let's make sure.

The man puts the hat on and walks up and down.

You see, you see, cries the man, it does nothing for me; I was only trying to be nice to the hatter, and the train was just pulling out, I had to run . . .

The police are of the opinion that the hat isn't all that bad . . . Perhaps a feather, a little work and it would be quite becoming . . .

No no, it's just not me! cries the man.

As the police discuss the hat the man whispers behind his hand to the collapsed building, oh, please get up.

And then he says to the police, no no, my dear cops, in the city where I come from, I forget its name, this hat would be considered an assault against the highest aspirations of mankind . . . The hatter, a true opportunist, taking every advantage of my kindness, noticing my lack of training in matters of taste . . . The train pulling out, having to run . . . An unfortunate birth

. . . All lack of talent and ambition . . . Forced into idleness for lack of proper amusement . . .

The police say, but the hat doesn't look all that bad . . . Perhaps a feather . . . ?

A man is bringing a cup of coffee to his face, tilting it to his mouth. It's historical, he thinks. He scratches his head: another historical event. He really ought to rest, he's making an awful lot of history this morning.

Oh my, now he's buttering toast, another piece of history is being made.

He wonders why it should have fallen on him to be so historical. Others probably just don't have it, he thinks, it is, after all, a talent.

He thinks one of his shoelaces needs tying. Oh well, another important historical event is about to take place. He just can't help it. Perhaps he's taking up too large an area of history? But he has to live, hasn't he? Toast needs buttering and he can't go around with one of his shoelaces needing to be tied, can he?

Certainly it's true, when the 20th century gets written in full it will be mainly about him. That's the way the cooky crumbles — ah, there's a phrase that'll be quoted for centuries to come.

Self-conscious? A little; how can one help it with all those yet-to-be-born eyes of the future watching him?

Uh oh, he feels another historical event coming . . . Ah, there it is, a cup of coffee approaching his face at the end of his arm. If only they could catch it on film, how much it would mean to the future.

Oops, spilled it all over his lap. One of those historical accidents that will influence the next thousand years; unpredictable, and really rather uncomfortable . . . But history is never easy, he thinks . . .

There is a room in a house where people keep crowding in. They are willing to stand pressed against strangers; and still they keep pressing into the room. They find it difficult to breathe; it is so moist, so uncomfortably moist . . .

No one on the street would realize that this house, quite an ordinary one, has a room totally packed with strangers. And so anyone might, and usually does, enter the house just to make sure that his wild speculation, that perhaps there is such a room, is totally untrue.

And when anyone passing the house, and then speculating on the possibility of such a room, discovers that, in fact, there is such a room entirely packed with standing people, he thinks there's something to it, and also forces himself into the room.

Now people are on the shoulders of others, their heads bowed under the ceiling. Nobody wants to miss out on what everybody else seems to be waiting for.

When the householder comes home and finds one of his rooms entirely packed with people, as if it were a public conveyance, he says, this cannot be, not in my house. And so he closes the door with all the people inside, who take this as a sign that something is about to begin, something exceedingly worthwhile; else, why have all these other people waited in the moist heat, in these crowded conditions? . . . Hard to breathe and all. . . .

The householder closes the door on the room in full knowledge that nothing of value, in spite even of expectant crowds, ever happens in his house. . . . A dead end, a closed tunnel, which he enters and reenters like a foot stubbed endless times into a shoe: The house that walks the night through the dreamless dark. . . .

I dream I have already awakened. I begin to prepare myself for the street.

I am ready, but suddenly I begin to cry.

The telephone rings. Still crying, I answer it. The voice at the other end is also crying, and I cannot make out what it is trying to say. And so we cry back and forth over the telephone to each other . . .

As I cry and listen to the crying in the telephone I look out of the window, and see all the people on the street crying. At least I'm not abnormal, I think to myself as I bawl even louder.

Then someone knocks at the door. I nod in the direction of the door, and whoever it is comes in, as though sensing my affirmative nod without seeing it. He is crying. Through his sobs he asks for a handkerchief. Still on the telephone, I tap my breast pocket, indicating a handkerchief. He reaches for it, but doesn't quite make it, and falls on my shoulder with desperate weeping.

Meanwhile, the person on the telephone continues his bawling and sobbing.

Now that the door is open people start to wander in from the street, beating their bosoms with grief, shuddering, their hands to their mouths; some even finding words, too bad, too bad, unbearable &c.

And suddenly, seeing all these people weeping as if weeping were normal behavior, I start to laugh. I cannot control it. It is suddenly so funny seeing all these people weeping.

And then they, noticing my laughter, sheepishly begin to grin through their tears. And one by one they break into amused laughter; roaring, ha ha, haw haw! Even the voice on the telephone is laughing.

Then, just as suddenly, I am crying again, and so is everybody else.

And then, I am laughing again, and again so is everybody else.

And then we are crying; and then we are laughing, on and on . . .

JOURNEY FOR AN OLD FELLOW

Can the old fellow get out of the kitchen? It is an arduous journey which will take him through those remarkable conversations of the dining room; and through the living room, where murder is so common that to even notice it proves one the amateur . . . Then the hallway and the stairs to the upstairs of dark bedrooms where boats rock at their moorings . . . Out through the walls grown translucent with moonlight, into a marble world of sheep grazing on the hills of the night . . .

THE LARGE THING

A large thing comes in.

Go out, Large Thing, says someone.

The Large Thing goes out, and comes in again.

Go out, Large Thing, and stay out, says someone.

The Large Thing goes out, and stays out.

Then that same someone who has been ordering the Large Thing out begins to be lonely, and says, come in, Large Thing.

But when the Large Thing is in, that same someone decides it would be better if the Large Thing would go out.

Go out, Large Thing, says this same someone.

The Large Thing goes out.

Oh, why did I say that? says the someone, who begins to be lonely again.

But meanwhile the Large Thing has come back in anyway.

Good, I was just about to call you back, says the same someone to the Large Thing.

A clown destroys a large liver which has been growing in his room for several years.

It began from a small blood stain on his wall, and has grown into a huge wet purple mattress bulging over his bed and make-up table. It is smothering his room, his elbow pokes into it when he sits to put his grease paint on; the covers of his bed are stuck under its weight.

He sticks the point of his funny parasol into it. It replies with a bloody cough.

He sticks the point of his funny parasol into it again, and it replies with a bloody fart.

Now he's into it, he's breaking it loose, prying it away from the wall with the handle of his funny parasol. It falls bleeding and breaking on everything; pieces of liver scattered all over the room . . .

Now dwarves are at his door shouting for the answer to the riddle of the Sphinx.

Please, I'm not ready, shouts the clown.

Then the fat lady's foot comes through the ceiling.

She must have eaten something . . .

The thin man is in the hall talking to the dwarves; he's going to try to squeeze through the keyhole.

Now the strong man is there, and he is offering to break the door down.

They have an elephant in the hall.

The circus manager is there, he's saying that if the clown doesn't open the door the building will have to be burned down.

The clown is wondering why the circus manager thinks the building will have to be burned down.

He hears the circus manager ordering someone to get some matches.

The dwarves are complaining that the clown hasn't answered the riddle of the Sphinx yet.

The fat lady's other foot comes through the ceiling. She must have eaten something else . . .

The thin man has forced one of his feet through the keyhole . . .

At the end, laughter and applause . . .

The clown curtsies, and begins to destroy a large liver again . . .

An official document blows through a forest between the trees over the heads of the picnickers.

It is the end of summer, and there is only the snow to be looked forward to. The photosynthetic world is collapsing.

Those who have been picnicking all summer in the forest see that their food has gone bad. The blackberry jam is tar, the picnic baskets are full of bones wrapped in old newspapers.

A young man turns to his sweetheart. She's an old woman with white hair; her head bobs on her neck.

The picnickers try to catch the document as it flies over their heads. But the wind carries it away.

What is written on it is that *the summer is over* . . .

THE LONELY EVENINGS OF DOCTOR FUNNYPERSON

Doctor Funnyperson likes bathroom furniture. For chairs he has toilets. His house looks like a public bathroom.

Lately the lonely Doctor Funnyperson is spending the evenings flushing his toilets; even as he studies the problem, why it is he would like to hurt someone.

Meanwhile he occupies the lonely evenings flushing his toilets one by one . . .

THE LONELY TRAVELER

He's a lonely traveler, and finds companion in the road; a chance meeting, seeing as how they were both going the same way.

. . . Only, the road had already arrived at its end; like a long snake, its eyes closed in the distance, asleep . . .

They're making a movie. But they've got it all wrong. The hero is supposed to be standing triumphantly on the deck of a ship, but instead is standing on scaffold about to be hanged.

The heroine is supposed to be embracing the hero on the deck of that same ship, but instead is being strapped down for an electric shock treatment.

Crowds of peasants who long for democracy, and are supposed to be celebrating the death of a tyrant, are, in fact, carrying that same tyrant on their shoulders, declaring him the savior of the people.

The director doesn't know what's gone wrong. The producer is very upset.

The stunt man keeps asking, now? as he flips and falls on his head.

Meanwhile a herd of elephants stampedes through central casting; and fake flood waters are really flooding the set.

The stunt man asks again, now? and again flips and falls on his head.

The director, scratching his head, says, perhaps the electric shock should be changed to insulin . . . ?

Are you sure? asks the producer.

No, but we might just as well try it. . . . And, by the way, that stunt man's not very good, is he?

A MAN WHO MAKES TEARS

There was a man who made things because he was lonely.
And so he made tears, which he thinks are tiny examples of
the mystery that is large enough at times to swallow whole
ships, and to be the road of the great whales. . . .

The man makes tears which he thinks come out of his
eyes from the memory of ponds and oceans. And he thinks
they are the tears of a marionette whose head is a jug of water
with a sad face painted on it. . . .

The officers go into the monkey house and arrest monkey-Jim. The zoo keeper, trying to be as poignant as he can, says, why are you putting handcuffs on monkey-Jim?

I'm sorry, but we have an arrest warrant on monkey-Jim.

Oh, but that's not monkey-Jim, that's monkey-Charlie.

Well, where is monkey-Jim?

That's monkey-Jim—no, *that's* monkey-Jim . . . No, wait, *that* one's monkey-Jim . . . Sorry, that's monkey-Sam. There're too many monkeys, I can't tell which one is monkey-Jim.

Well, we'll just pick one at random, they all look alike, who's to know the difference?

But they all have names. If you take monkey-Elmer and call him monkey-Jim he'll think you're talking to somebody over his shoulder and won't confess. If you happen to take monkey-Overstreet the same thing'll happen.

Yes, that's true, say the officers, that's no fun. No one can expect monkey-Elmer or monkey-Overstreet to confess to monkey-Jim's crime . . . unless we torture them. Yeah, but that kind of a confession never seems sincere; sincerity is really important with confessions. . . .

Well, officers, what can be done?

I guess we'll just have to torture monkey-Elmer. . . .

You're not going to leave monkey-Overstreet out, are you?

The officers say among themselves, we can't leave monkey-Overstreet out, not after building up his hopes. . . . Okay, they say, monkey-Overstreet can confess to monkey-Jim's crimes, too.

Oh, what a lovely surprise for monkey-Overstreet!

THE NEARSIGHTED RICH MAN

A nearsighted rich man has all the windows in his house ground to his optical prescription.

He remains rich and nearsighted . . .

There is an audience that sits like a fat man waiting for his dinner.

The lights are dimming, he anticipates, he salivates. . . .

And yet, on the street in back of this theater is another theater, where another audience also sits like a fat man awaiting his dinner. There the lights are also dimming. . . .

But when the curtains part in both theaters they turn out to be the same curtains, and both audiences sit facing each other, each expecting the other is part of the play it has come to see.

And so the audiences wait, each like a fat man facing another fat man, both becoming nutritionally impatient.

Now it is occurring to both audiences that the other audience is sitting on its stage, displacing the area of its expectation; so that two fat men are breaking into a rage: thousands of fingers attached to the bodies of screaming mouths rush greedily at the other, each seeing the other as the impediment of his rightful portion. Men and women screaming and crying, as though life deprived of the ambitions of pleasure were little worth the living; no middle ground of simple satisfaction rooted in any of the wholesome habits. . . .

They wave their theater tickets and scream, soiling their clothes. They chew on the curtains, on the seats, nipping and barking at the rug, as if the fumes of previous plays, like old cigarette smoke, might yet be tasted in the cloth objects of the theater.

48

Finally the curtains close. They return to their seats and applaud. One audience rises to its feet crying, bravo, bravo, while the curtains part and the facing audience stands and bows. Then this is reversed, and then reversed again; until at last, like two fat men having finished their dinners, each audience files out of its side of the double theater . . .

The ceiling closes heaven like a door. This old man is local to wall and ceiling, the drawn curtains and the fire in his hearth . . .

His son struggles in the dark above the house, like a rubber boot tumbled and driven in a river. The old man wonders if it is not chimney smoke that creates the tortured ghost.

The old man, who is himself dead but for memory of when he lived, sits then remembering when he was not dead in ghost summers fading like old photographs where shadow and light become less different all the time, all the time, until at last they'll not be different . . .

The old man makes a high note with his voice; holds it; thinks he can hold it indefinitely. It is not a sound usual to the range of his voice or desire. It is the sound of a violin string where a bow of seeming infinite length is drawn on it through the hours of the night.

It is not like a scream that would fill the room with red bits of flesh. It is a high-pitched yellow beam, eeeeeeeee, that goes on and on, neither falling nor rising, without use or emotional intent.

And he wonders why he has never done this before . . . Being so near death, or so far from life; being, as it were, without the desire for either life or death; being between, without leaning one way or the other—why had he never found this high-pitched note in himself before, this one which he holds through the night?

His son struggles in the dark above the house like chimney smoke tumbled and driven in the wind ... Memory, which is clogged with death and illusion, with thousands of leaves which the mind's eye records as areas of summer ... All this and more, coffee cups and spoons, doors that opened and closed, all the streets and roads that were at last one, roof slope and shadow, the soft coat of twilight over the day ... And the high note continues, even as the first pale light begins to describe the earth again ...

I have just returned from my summer home in the country. I admit a certain amount of time has elapsed, it usually does. Every time one turns time has slipped a little. No hope for it. . . .

I have just returned from my summer home in the country. Did I say this before?

I have just returned from my summer home in the country. I have the strangest feeling of having said this before. . . . Perhaps a little déjà vu . . . ?

But, to get on, I have just returned from my summer home in the country. Time has been erecting its barriers which, to be sure, are soft enough, and may be expressed as a kind of mental geography of distance. Human psychology, of course, may be the entire cause of this invisible appearance which time slowly makes upon the mind, the awareness of having wasted one's life. . . .

I have just returned from my summer home in the country. I have just returned from my . . . Didn't I just say this?

I have just returned from my summer home in the country. This sounds so familiar, like the refrain of a memory buried so deeply that only its ornament shows. . . . It is ornamental, isn't it?

How do I do it? It just comes to me. Remarkable, isn't it? I mean the ornament of it. The fact is I live in the country and only pretend to be returning to my city apartment after a summer at my country home. It gives geographical significance, an animal with regular migrations. . . .

I have just returned from my summer home in the country to resume a literary career at my New York City address.

I have just returned from my summer home in the country. Do you still like the ornament? Would you like to hear it again?

All right, once more, and then I'm quits: I have just returned from my summer home in the country. . . . Somehow this still sounds so familiar . . .

A king had dropped his crown—oh quite by accident, he screamed, for it likely foretells the fall of the king's pants, scattering his perfection into the eyes of lusting peasants.

The crown was broken. His wife, the female king, cried, it's my crown which you broke.

Oh, really? he screamed, I must have put it on by accident; I thought it was too small. Good thing it wasn't mine, yours is just a silly old girl's crown. Now you'll have to go down to the kitchen and clean pots.

No no, I will wear the king's crown, which makes me the king, she screamed.

Oh no, that's only for the king to wear; the king wears the king's crown; other than that is a perversion, you lesbian, he screamed.

You're the queer, wearing a lady's crown, you transvestite, screamed the queen.

But you see I instinctively threw it off, because underneath my wayward delight is the true instinct, he screamed.

Too late, too late, because I am wearing the king's crown: and in that we are married, and in that the wearer of the king's crown is automatically the king, you are now the queen who broke her crown like a typically silly woman who doesn't quite realize the value of things, screamed the queen.

I will not play this naughty game, he screamed, and I shall have you beheaded if you cannot come to terms with your disquiet.

I shall have you beheaded if you cannot come to terms with your disquiet, she screamed.

No no, I shall have you beheaded if you cannot come to terms with your disquiet, he screamed.

How dare you? It is I that have people beheaded when they cannot come to terms with their disquiet, she screamed.

I shall most certainly require that you be beheaded if you refuse to come to terms with your disquiet, he screamed.

Quiet, she screamed.

I said I want silence, he screamed.

A page boy came and said, sirs, shall I bring your mouth-plugs now?

Of course, screamed the king and queen; are you blind, can't you see our mouths are completely out of whack?

It was the last Thursday of November, and a large turkey had been murdered . . .

They say he was up in bed reading a cookbook just before sleep. They say he had just handled his pocket watch; perhaps to wind it and see the time. There was a feather caught on the winding stem.

On the table next to the bed was an open ink jar with a quill pen stuck in it. The turkey evidently had been marking a recipe in the cookbook for oyster stuffing. . . .

His head, still wearing its sleeping cap, was on the pillow. The body had obviously been dragged through the window and across the yard through the snow. . . .

The investigation has been postponed because of the holiday; most of the police will be having Thanksgiving dinner with their families. . . .

THE PARENTAL DECISION

A man splits into two who are an old woman and an old man.

They must be his parents. But where is the man? Perhaps he gave his life for them . . .

I ask the old couple if they've seen their son.

The old woman says, we've decided not to have any children.

A man opening a walnut shell finds a tiny unborn monkey; thinks he must be mistaken, the walnut was not a walnut, but a monkey egg.

. . . Monkeys lay eggs; of course they do because they live in trees like birds. They are really birds, flightless birds like ostriches.

He opens another walnut and finds a walnut inside. Hmmm, he says, the monkey egg has a walnut inside; that's funny. . . . Maybe this is really a walnut? . . . No, it can't be because the first walnut was a monkey egg, which makes this walnut wrong if it is a walnut.

Please don't be a walnut, he says to the walnut.

But just then the great clock of the universe shows that it's time for the earth to end, even as it shows that the time has come for other things to begin.

The man says, just before the clock strikes, please don't be a walnut. . . .

PLUNK PLUNK PLUNK

There is an old man who makes love to a bicycle in a bed where his wife sleeps. The old hands that have become like thick paws play the spokes for the music of the lyre: Plunk plunk plunk. . . .

But he cannot find the bicycle's vagina. Perhaps it's up under the seat. He thinks it's up under the seat—anatomically it should be!

And the old hands that have become like thick paws are all over the bicycle searching; chain grease on the sheets of the bed; the back wheel spins against the sheet, hissing and sighing. . . . The thin cold arms of the handlebars almost embrace. . . .

Embrace me! cries the old man.

His wife comes awake and says, why don't you work on that in the morning?

No no, I've almost got it working!

But how can you see in the dark?

I can feel it! I can feel it! he cries.

Get that dirty bicycle out of our bed!

No no, please, mommy!

I've never heard of anything so silly, using a bed for a bicycle shop, she says.

I can't find the vagina, cries the old man.

I have it, whispers the old woman.

Give it back, it belongs to my wife! cries the old man.

I am your wife, sighs the old woman.

You're my wife . . . ?

I thought you knew. . . .

But what about the bicycle's vagina? !

Get that bicycle out of our bed, this is not a bicycle shop! screams the old woman.

59

The old man whose hands have become like thick paws begins once more to play the bicycle's spokes for the music of the lyre: Plunk plunk plunk. . . .

And so of the night, these two in bed, and old man and an old woman; he, embracing a bicycle, she, waking every so often complaining that their bed is not a bicycle shop. . . .

Plunk plunk plunk. . . .

A doctor is called to a house where a woman is about to have a baby. But when the doctor gets there he feels a little pregnant himself, and asks the woman's husband to call another doctor.

The woman's husband also looks a little bloated.

The doctor says, hey, you're not pregnant too, are you?

Well, Doctor, it's true, I have been feeling a little pregnant of late. Maybe I caught it from my wife?

When the second doctor arrives it's discovered that he's also pregnant . . .

And so the woman who is about to have a baby listens far into the night as three men argue about names for their own unborn children, which they fully expect will be sons . . .

This is the house of the closet-man. There are no rooms, just hallways and closets.

Things happen in rooms. He does not like things to happen.

. . . Closets, you take things out of closets, you put things into closets, and nothing happens . . .

Why do you have such a strange house?

I am the closet-man, I am either going or coming, and I am never sad.

But why do you have such a strange house?

I am never sad . . .

She serves delicious shoe for dinner with a side order of stockings and girdle.

A hungry old man consumes her wardrobe.

She is serving underwear smothered in sweat and lack of bathing, slipping off her backside in an old rooming house where someone knows the back way to her vagina—loves it that way! He is such an animal!

Oh, how she rolls her stockings into doughnuts on her ankles!

The old man wants her breasts: where are they, where are they?!

On my chest, where else?

Yes yes, of course. And so he has sex between her breasts.

He is rolling in her underwear, asking where she keeps her mouth—her rectum!—Wants one of the doughnuts on her ankles with coffee in her shoe!

He wipes his mouth and says, it's one of the best rooming house dinners he's ever had. . .

. . . Someday it's stuffed shoes, stuffed with her own feet, served on a strange street where she is at last finding happiness way in the distance. . . .

THE SCREAM

In a window is a head full of stairways where people are walking up and down carrying trays of potted plants.

And in that head are stairways where people move up and down carrying bowls of steaming porridge; stairways where people move up and down carrying bowls of mock turtle soup. . . .

And then all at once all the people carrying pails of mutton fat up and down the stairways stop and begin to scream . . .

And all at once the head in the window opens its mouth and all the people on the stairways scream . . .

He struggles out of a closet where his mother had hung him forty years ago.

She didn't understand children; she probably thought he was something made of cloth.

He thinks he has waited long enough for her to understand children, even though he is no longer a child.

After forty years a man has a right to seek the hallway; after all, he might even hope for the front door—and who knows, perhaps even a Nobel Prize for patience!

From the front porch he sees that the midday sky is darker than he remembered it; the green of the lawn and trees has also darkened: too many nights, too many coats of varnish . . .

This is not the same summer, the color is gone. . . .

. . . That little boy who is always passing the house with his wagon has turned into a little old man collecting garbage. . . .

When he sleeps in his chair, his hands clasped on his belly—perhaps he snores a little, is it wrong?—chains of dark little ants stream up and down his nostrils transporting grains of his mind away.

This he tells Dr. Graciousness, who smiles graciously at such a quaint telling of one losing his mind, describing that same loss of mind in such a quaint way.

But, Dr. Graciousness, what am I to do? asks the man.

Dr. Graciousness continues to smile.

You have a very gracious smile, Dr. Graciousness, but what am I to do?

But Dr. Graciousness only continues to smile.

I admit your smile is a most gracious one, Dr. Graciousness, but what am I to do?

The answer is very simple, yours is the sweet madness, says the smiling Dr. Graciousness at last, you must put your sugar in a bowl with a cover on it . . .

THE TAXI

One night in the dark I phone for a taxi. Immediately a taxi crashes through the wall; never mind that my room is on the third floor, or that the yellow driver is really a cluster of canaries arranged in the shape of a driver, who flutters apart, streaming from the windows of the taxi in yellow fountains . . .

Realizing that I am in the midst of something splendid I reach for the phone and cancel the taxi: All the canaries flow back into the taxi and assemble themselves into a cluster shaped like a man. The taxi backs through the wall, and the wall repairs . . .

But I cannot stop what is happening, I am already reaching for the phone to call a taxi, which is already beginning to crash through the wall with its yellow driver already beginning to flutter apart . . .

... So it is given: we follow as through a tunnel down through the trees into the earth, where the dead swim cleansed of the world; innocent in undiscovered desire ...

Chains of events hold between points, bridges that are not for the traveler, but for the seer, for whom such bridges are unnecessary ...

The porridge on the table longs for the ceiling, dreaming of new plasticities ...

The window watches with all its meadows and rivers, its trees leaning in the wind to see more fully ...

Everything is made of time, and we go out in waves, accumulating around ourselves in halos of dust; the borders bleeding each into the other; the tearing and merging of clouds ...

THROUGH THE DARKNESS OF SLEEP

In sleep: softly, softly, angel soldiers mob us with their brutal wings; stepping from the clouds they break through the attic like divers into a sunken ship.

A handful of shingles they hold, leafing through them like the pages of our lives; the book of the roof: here is the legend of the moss and the weather, and here the story of the overturned ship, sunken, barnacled by the markings of birds. . . .

. . . We are to be led away, one by one, through the darkness of sleep, through the mica glitter of stars, down the stairways of our beds, into the roots of trees . . . slowly surrendering, tossing and turning through centuries of darkness. . . .

A woman thinks she must cook her cat today . . .

Suddenly tears, like theater glycerin, seep up out of her ducts and down her cheeks. She thinks of a plague that might overtake the birds, causing all the birds of the world to die . . . They are raked up like leaves . . . In a few weeks humankind forgets that there ever were birds on earth. . . .

The sweet hot lachrymal tide once more overflows as she thinks of music being torn and scattered by the wind; musicians overtaken by sudden flood; an earthquake finally destroying the house of music. . . .

Clouds, she thinks of clouds, dark like caves; holes where people wander, having lost their minds; there, those who do evil ride bicycles in mockery of those that stumble forward, mindless, like the blind with broken butterfly hands. . . .

She thinks she must cook her cat today. . . . Set it on fire! Squeeze it in the door! . . . This to keep herself from screaming. . . .

... So the idiot is led in and given a key and asked to unlock the chain around his neck. This is done many times, perhaps for a lifetime. If he is once able to unlock the chain he is raised to imbecile, and released from that same chain whose unlocking proves the idiot to be an imbecile.

At this all the other imbeciles and idiots at the Vegetable House are given holiday from their mental deficiencies to celebrate one who has earned imbecile from idiot; at the end of which, of course, the celebrants are returned to their former omissions.

Should the imbecile who has made idiot then make moron, and then, having learned a good habit, go on to *average* ... But he doesn't stop, now he's above average, he's even to be considered bright—very bright; he's entering the lower levels of the genius class—he makes full genius!

Of course the keepers at the Vegetable House are somewhat amazed, they cannot tell whether to consider this a victory or a defeat. To make sure they relock the chain around the neck of the genius, explaining that it is mere form, a little red tape, ha ha, just one of those things, a precaution, don't you know, the authorities require ... The state permits ... The Board of Alcohol Control, and all that, foreign relations, state department, forms to be filled out, requirements to be met ... The mayor's wife, considerations, favors, judgeships, certain kickbacks, political plums, passes, franchises, fortunes made overnight, oil interests, foreign requests, travel abroad, visits in

71

the cool of the evening, a reprieve from the governor, a presidential pardon ... And not to forget a certain king who stumbled ... Forms, forms, mere form, form for its own sake....
Are you listening? ...

THE WEATHER, FOR ONE THING ...

A summer morning. In a solarium a young man plays a piano.

How green and saved seems the world!

But the music stops. And the young man is found bent forward at the piano, his hands, still on the keys, melted like drippings of wax. His head, a shapeless thing, hangs down from his collar ...

Someone touches his shoulder as if to awaken him; the young man topples and slides to the floor.

Something is broken, a waxy substance begins to seep out of the ends of his trousers and sleeves; as though he exhaled from a deep breath, his clothes flattening, the white substance gathering in pools on the floor ...

The sun is suddenly covered by clouds, the solarium is dark. Rain is beginning to fall; coming harder, beating on the glass.

Something seems so wrong now. What, exactly, no one can quite place. Someone offers the weather, for one thing ... Yes, that could be it; the radio predicted sunshine ... and now this awful rain ...